Stories from Islam

Ayub gets His Riches Back

Ziya Us Salam

Om KIDZ
An imprint of Om Books International

One evening, Salman was surprised to hear
his grandmother talking to herself.

“Who are you talking to grandmother?”
Salman peeped into her room but found no one else.

"I am not talking to anyone, Salman. I was reading aloud the story of Prophet Ayub, who is mentioned many times in the Quran. Would you like to know his story?"

"Of course, I would, Grandma!" said Salman. "Tell me his story."

"Well," said Rasheeda. "He was a rich man. Unfortunately, he fell very ill. Sores and wounds covered his body.

"The people of his town sent him away, fearing that his disease would spread to others. Nobody stayed with him except his wife, who looked after him with love and care.

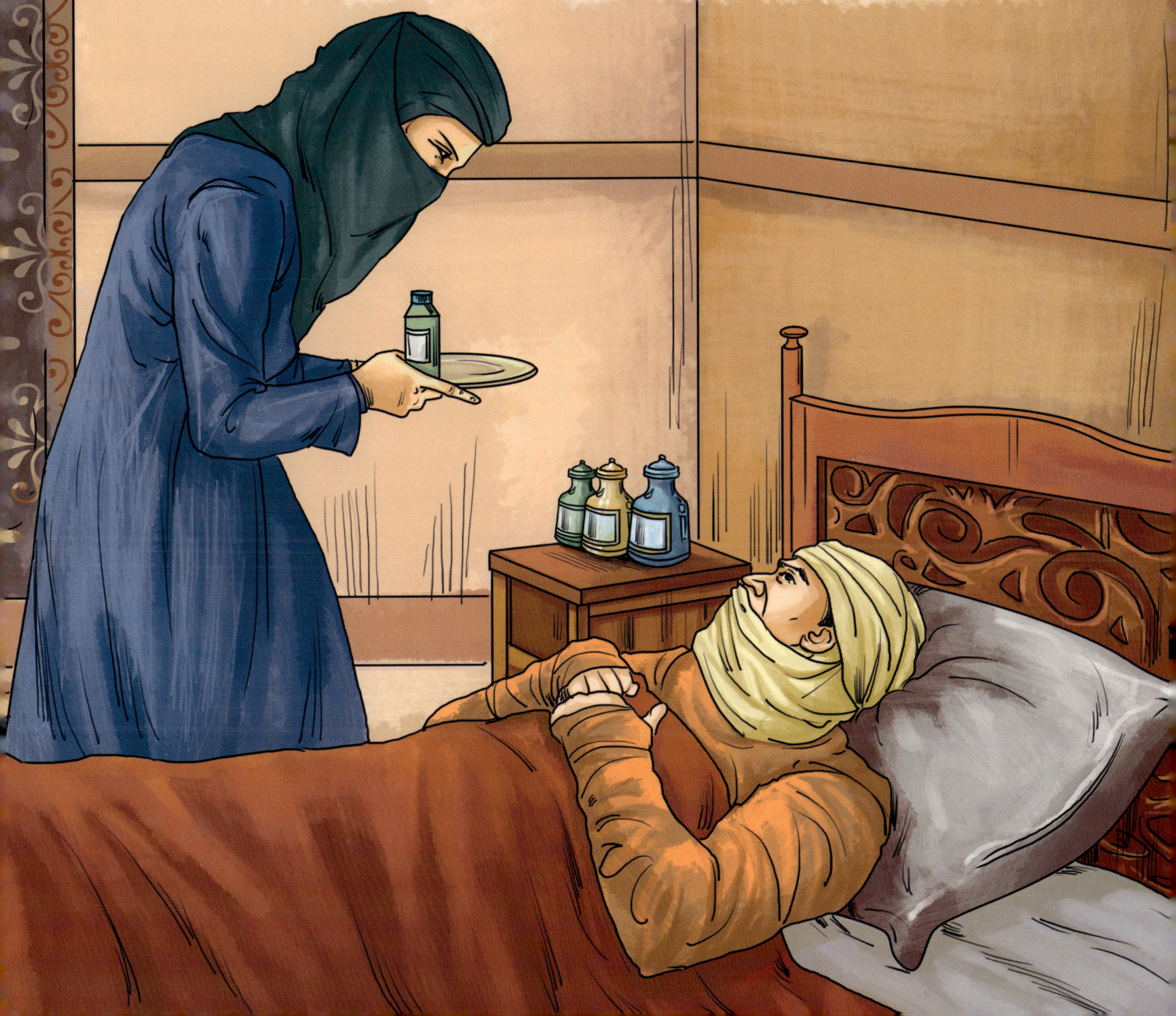

“His treatment was long and very expensive. Slowly, he started losing his riches due to the cost of his medicines.

"Yet, he did not recover. He felt pain in his whole body. He could hardly move due to the pain."

"Did he ever recover, then?" Salman asked.

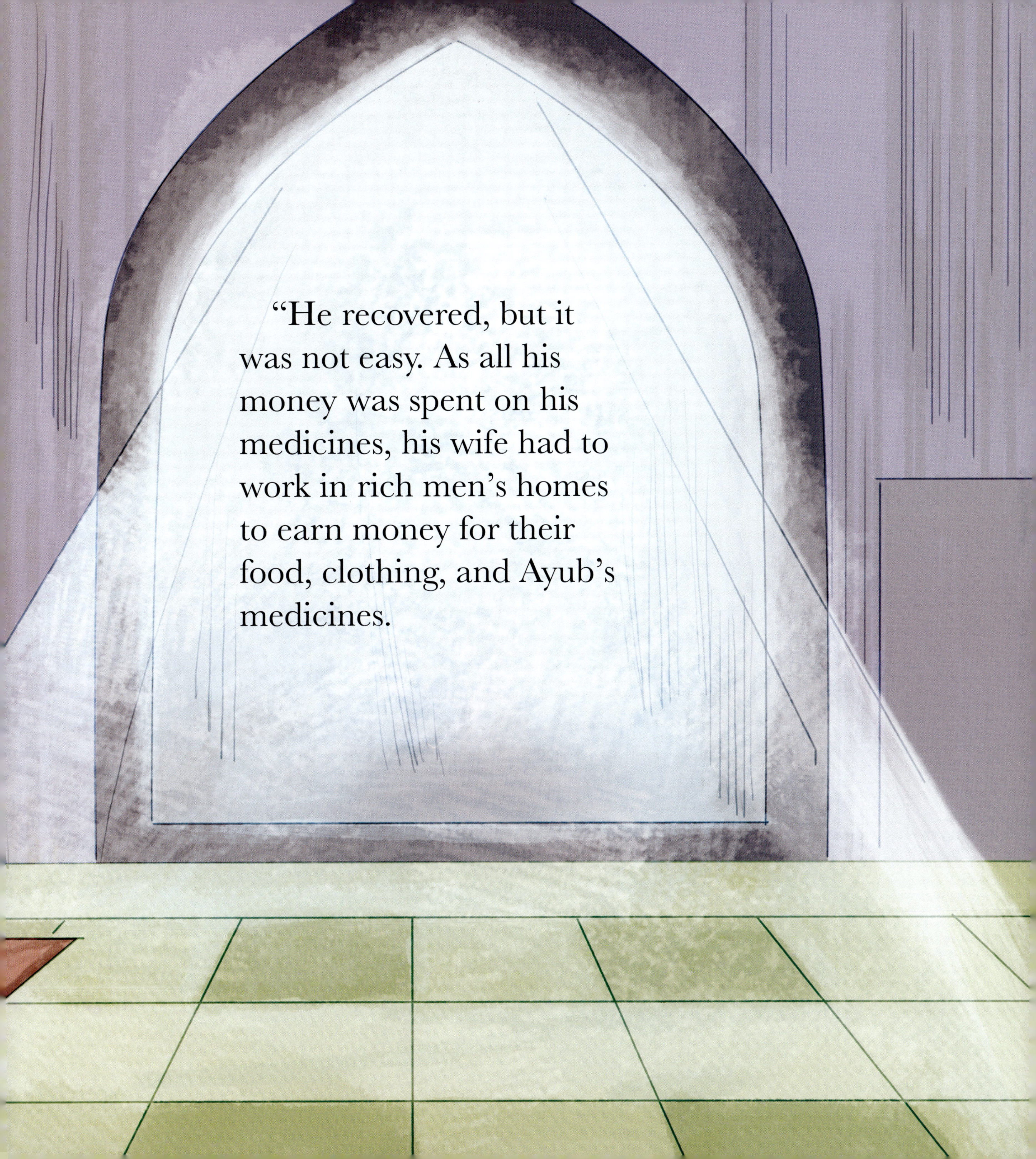

"He recovered, but it was not easy. As all his money was spent on his medicines, his wife had to work in rich men's homes to earn money for their food, clothing, and Ayub's medicines.

"Ayub remained patient through all this, and never lost faith in Allah. He prayed to Allah to end his troubles.

“One day he was sitting outside the town, praying. His wife was away at work. Suddenly, he heard a voice telling him to strike the land with this foot. Believing it to be Allah’s will, Ayub struck the ground.

"Immediately, water gushed out of the place where his foot had struck. Ayub drank the water, then washed himself with it. As he cleaned his body, all his sores disappeared. He became healthy again. Allah had rewarded him for his patience.

"He got his riches back, and was reunited with his family. His wife did not have to work in rich men's homes anymore. This reward, Allah gave to Ayub for being patient," said Rasheeda.

"So, if we have a problem, we must be patient as Allah will help us," Salman said, happy to have understood the moral of the story.